I0420580

Deepening Nigeria's Democracy;
Issues and Challenges before the National Conference

©Orchid Publishers,
Port Harcourt, Nigeria, 2015

Deepening Nigeria's Democracy; Issues and Challenges before the
National Conference, 2015
©Orike Ben Didi

ISBN-13: 978-1518767845
Made in the USA by Charleston, SC

Contents

Introduction

The search for the political and economic future of Nigeria is important to the Black Race. This is not just because Nigeria appropriates the highest concentration of black people anywhere in the world, but more because of the enormous human and material resources available for the positive transformation of the African continent. This has not been possible due to the trajectory of Nigeria's history and the faulty social and political structures which have impeded the realization the country's full potentials.

The search for viable socio-political structures translated to a constant recourse through constitutional conferences towards the attainment of a better constitution. The search which commenced during the pre-independence period is still on-going and may not end in the next few decades. The 2014 National Conference is one set of events towards the making of a lasting constitution for Nigeria.

In this presentation the deepening of Nigeria's democracy was considered in the context of the outcomes of the issues and challenges projected before, during and after the national conference of 2014 held in Abuja, the capital of the country.

The publication of the lecture was initially discounted in favour of newspaper entries. Unfortunately, the events which closely followed the conference (like the 2015 general elections, both the campaigns and the aftermath of the elections in Nigeria) resurrected the turbulent issues that were discussed in the lecture, hence the need to publish it in the form in which it appears here.

It is my hope that this contribution to the debate on structure and forms of the Nigerian state in the face of the existing 'democratic' culture will also expand the robustness of our march towards a more viable future.

Orike Ben Didi
25 October, 2015
Takoradi, Ghana

Dedicated

To Dr. Isaac Asume Osuoka,
one of the conference participants whose yearning to change
Nigeria for good remains unending.

Acknowledgement

I am grateful to Mr. Chinedu Karl Uchegbu who facilitated the invitation and read through the lecture before its actual presentation. I am equally grateful to Dr. Chidi Eze who continued communication with me and anchored the presentation session proper. I also wish to thank the members of De Norsemen Klub International and their then National President Mr. Victor Okiri for giving me the opportunity and freedom to speak my mind about our collective malaise. I will also remain grateful for the attention of participants at the 14th General Assembly lecture of the DNKI held in Awka, Nigeria. Their responses in forms of questions and comments after the lecture showed so much concern for the future of Nigeria and the black race.

**Deepening Nigeria's Democracy;
Issues and Challenges before the National Conference*.**

*The national conference of 2014

<u>Deepening Nigeria's Democracy;</u>

<u>Issues and Challenges before the National Conference.</u>

Lecture Delivered at the 14th General Assembly

of the De Norsemen Klub International

Held at Joburg Hotels, Awka on the 24th of May, 2014.

Orike Didi, PhD

I stand on existing protocols.

Introduction:

I must state in the first course that I am happy to be here today to share some thoughts and ideas which are not akin to just me, but all of us. I say this because I believe that thoughts are like a disease which infects whoever places himself in the condition of who had suffered from the disease earlier, especially if the former and later persons have the same immunity level. An increased immunity level could, for me, be equivalent to an inverted corollary of ideological consciousness.

Let me also state that it is now a common occurrence to see Nigerians complain about their country and leaders. It is just as normal as breathing in air. And I have for a long time come to the conclusion that most Nigerians when asked to open, at random, a book in the Bible will most likely open to the Book of Lamentations. Therefore, if you see me complain about and criticize our leaders here, just understand that I am still a Nigerian.

Before I go into what I am here to discuss today, let me also state that many Nigerians have given up on the country. With the level of decay of the society's institutions and the impunity that is concomitant with our political and social spaces many believe that Nigeria cannot fulfill its role in liberating the black race from poverty and disease. After all, it is difficult for a man who is not free to free other people.

For the period of this presentation we will consider that we are freemen, and free men are those who define what they are free from. Today, we are free from fear! Today we will also think of how to free ourselves and our country from poverty and want - at least on paper. There will be no legal penalties for the thoughts and opinions we are going to express here.

Some participants in this conference will expect me to talk about the Boko Haram menace, the failure of the Nigerian defence forces to check their onslaught on our polity, the inability of security agents in freeing the kidnapped 234 school girls of Chibok in Bornu State, the audacity of the 'conflict Republic' of 'Sambisa' and her renegade 'head of state', Malam Abubakar Shekau. Some others will expect me to talk about the marginalization debate of the South East and under-representation of the population of the area in vital institutions of society, or the confusion of development in the Niger Delta area and emerging false consciousness which has reduced the so-called Niger Delta struggle to hostage taking rackets. Still, others will expect to hear of the agricultural crises in the middle belt and the betrayal of governance and the indigene /settler quagmire in the area, and the ruling class crises in the West and the illusion of advancement. Some will still expect me to talk about extreme poverty in the North and the dislocated aims of the leaders there. I am definitely not here to talk about these issues for they are mere symptoms of a debilitating disease. And like the late sage, Chief Obafemi Awolowo will say 'problems are like plants, they have roots.' We should rather concern ourselves with the root causes of problems and less with the symptoms. So, while I will, from time to time, make references to these issues I am not here to dwell on them.

Deepening Nigeria's Democracy?

When I was handed this topic I knew there will be some difficulty in wriggling through and out of it. It was like asking me to solve all of Nigeria's problems in one single presentation. It was like installing a president and asking him to solve the problem of corruption in one day, not minding the corruptive influences and personalities that rigged him into office. It is my take that as at this moment what we have is a mere civilian administration and not a democracy. So how do you all expect me to advance a project or process that is non-existent? How do we deepen democracy when its basic features are observed only in their misuse and abuse?

However, since we are trapped in the geographical space referred to as Nigeria for now and the load of analysis has been lifted from the ground unto the shoulders, we will attempt to take it to destination. I will request your help whenever the load gets too heavy and corrections whenever I make errors of judgment. After all it is our problem, hence we will attempt first at rationalizing the crisis.

Rationalizing the Nigerian Crisis

There is a fundamental indifference to rationalizing the Nigerian crisis and perhaps the Nigerian non-nation being. There has existed for a long time that temptation of a summary, the closest exit to and an apparent refusal to understand the dynamics of that 'geographical expression', the hoping that an escape from analysis will invest the body polity with a kind of morality. But morality as multiplied as it is today basically abbreviates an attempt at a conclusive analysis of the body and soul of an otherwise faulty entity, so failing in function to its constituents and so betraying in its role to the black man.

Nigeria as it is presently represented by its political and economic crafters is a non-nation. Across the country there are no shared values and no representative dream. Unknown to many individuals trapped in the geographical space referred to as Nigeria it is not the actions of the 'economic autonomists', 'ultra-religious purists' or 'regional self-determinationists', or even the self-confessed 'regional hegemonists' that clearly express the non-nation being of Nigeria. Some of these expressions and their militant degenerations are actually an appendage of a political variant seeking a face through a faceless medium. The others seem to emerge from some form of confused conjectures seeking to deceive themselves into believing that proper thinking is taking place. It is the actual mouthing by our leaders, especially in times of crisis and national independence celebrations, of the indivisibility of the Nigerian state that confirms in absolute terms the non-existence of a nation in the geographical space between the gulf of guinea and the lower Sudan. The looming non-existence of a nation is even more stated with the machinations of the Nigerian ruling classes; the admixture of corruptive personalities and tendencies, and democratic pretensions in an atmosphere of lamentation by the democracy-betrayed.

In the first place who needs democracy? Or more aptly put who needs this kind of democracy that has beautiful but complex characters like Obasanjo, Jonathan, Odili, Ibori, Amaechi, Orji Uzor Kalu, Tinubu, Okorocha, Ciroma, Atiku, Buhari, Olabode George, Kwakwanso, Babangida Aliyu, Bamanga Tukur and Ibrahim Babangida playing great roles? Who needs democracy with a lame-duck national assembly whose major plus is that some of its members have confessed to crime and the remnant membership is suspected of kleptocratic tendencies? Who needs a democracy with state assemblies whose memberships are on permanent leave of legislative duty, only reconvening once in a while to share raw cash under executive rubber stamp? Who needs a democracy with the ruling party very far from internal democracy and constantly at home with dictatorial machinations? Who needs a democracy with the judiciary in the dock accused of compromising itself and apparently sentenced to irrelevance by a combination of material possessions, raw cash and levers of power? Of what use is a democracy when elections are a declaration of war and voters and passers-by seasonal victims of collateral damage? Who needs a democracy with a confessed opposition permanently reasoning below its actions and whose political philosophy is definitely not differentiated from that of the ruling party, but still scream – CHANGE!? Definitely not this writer.

Each time I see Bernabas Gemade making contributions to the proceedings of the Senate I wonder what kind of progress his contributions will engender. Each time I see his face on national television I start to laugh and the only thing of value I remember he has done was as a million man dancer for Abacha's "democratic" ambition shrouded in the 'five fingers of a leprous hand'. At least his action then was of value to the late maximum ruler whose earth-shaking death ended a certain terrible brand of political experimentation. In the not too distant past I had also watched Senator Omisore make similar contributions to the proceedings of the Senate. Yes, this was a man who was being tried for the murder of the then Minister of Justice Bola Ige. But instead of sitting in jail or hanging from the noose, he was seated in the hallowed chambers making 'bloody' laws for Nigerians. While the late Justice Minister Bola Ige is yet to get justice Senator Omisore has re-emerged of late as the PDP gubernatorial flag bearer in Osun State and up till date no one has been held responsible for the death of Bola Ige. That is the nature of democracy in Nigeria. That is the nature of public morality in Nigeria – a situation where the scale tilts towards the 'killer takes all' and the victim gets blamed for being killed.

We could as well decide to leave out the dead (like Chuba Okadigbo and Evan(s) Enwerem) and the forgotten like Adolphus Wabara and Patricia Etteh and their tampering with public morality when they headed the national assembly. But what shall we say of the recently disgraced Dimeji Bankole, the erstwhile speaker of the House of Representatives? This was a man who was charged for stealing public funds while in office to the tune of twenty billion naira. With connections to some of the guardians of our 'umbrella' and 'family affair' democracy he walked home a free man and is freely enjoying his loot till this day. The last check on him either popped him up as planning to contest the gubernatorial elections in Ogun State or speaking to students of the University of Agriculture, Abeokuta on leadership issues. At the start of the 2012/2013 university's session, Honorable Dimeji Bankole was to state that the major problem of Nigeria is ''lack of adequate preparation for leadership, especially in public life'' which he identified as ''a critical missing link in the nation's search for solutions.'' This was a leader who was believed to have just finished mismanaging his office talking! Instead of keeping quiet while his corruption case was raging, he was busy manifesting the common parallel morality of many Nigerian public officials - bold faced shamelessness and inability to admit guilt even when caught red handed.

The recent national assembly bribery brouhaha finally put paid to the denials of members of the national assembly of corruption accusations. Farouk Lawan was caught on camera receiving bribe money and stuffing them in his pockets and under his cap, and later on television defending his corruption in the 'hallowed' chambers. He even agreed to have received part of the 620 million dollar bribe for a reason different from corruption. The populace concluded that the house was completely lawanized, which is a byword for being corrupted and those who said that the Farouk Lawan case will end in the 'umbrella way' were not wrong after all. The police have not gone beyond arresting the lawmaker, freeing him and letting him go home to sin no more. Does this not approximate the fact that crime ceases to be crime when the criminal is connected to certain principalities and characters representing the

Nigerian state? Does this not imply that our brand of democracy has been apprehended and is stuck in the dock facing judgment?

Of late we saw Olabode George talking about total war on corruption. The question is: if such a war is started and the judiciary is not manipulated to satisfy certain whims and caprices, who will be the first to be caught in its web? Who? Myself or Olabode George? I do not know what psychologists will call this kind of consciousness or morality?

But honestly speaking, what brand of human specimen do we expect in political offices when elections are a total declaration of war and bullets are ballot papers stuffed into boxes? How do we expect the 'elected' to represent us adequately when the electoral process is compromised in every of its steps? What brand of democracy do we intend to build when people who can contribute to development are schemed out of democratic institutions of society?

Nigerians have simply relapsed into some dangerous quietism, wished away the evil day, hoping that prayers to God or the multiplication of mosques and churches will vanquish all the man-made socio-economic problems of Nigeria. While miracles were distributed like free peanuts in some later-day Pentecostal churches and warped irreligious minds were indoctrinating adherents into violence in the quasi 'forest republic' of Sambisa everyone also knew that very serious socio-political problems with the most populous black nation in the world had come to a head. But these were mere symptoms. The main disease was poverty of the masses and the threat of ensuring ungovernability of the country by some Northern leaders who had either lost elections in the past and/or are interested in the national elections of 2015. The problems were so daunting that the president himself acknowledged that there was need for stakeholders of the public space to talk to themselves. This was the precursor to the ongoing national conference.

The National Conference

The National Conference came as a 2013 independence-day presidential largesse. It was unexpected because the president himself had in the past discounted the idea of a national conference. The president merely echoed the views of the Nigerian ruling classes who thought that with the presence of a national assembly, it was unnecessary to raise a national conference with seemingly similar constitution-making responsibilities.

Subsequently a 13-man conference Presidential Advisory Committee (PAC) chaired by Senator Okunrounmu was established with a seven-point terms of reference, some of which include; to advise government on the framework for the national dialogue by consulting widely with Nigerians and to submit a report in six weeks. The committee went round the different geo-political zones to feel the pulse of the country, taking suggestions from varied sources and eventually came out with a report of what the conference should look like.

The committee was inherently dissolved the moment the report was submitted to the presidency. The PAC's report was submitted and on the 30th of January, 2014 the modalities for the conference was made public by the Secretary to the Government of the Federation, Senator Ayim Pius Ayim. A total of 492 delegates were named as conferees and the leadership of the conference was vested on Justice Idris Kutigi, a retired Chief Justice of the Supreme Court of Nigeria. The conference was subsequently inaugurated on the 17th of February, 2014 at the National Judicial Institute, Abuja with President Goodluck Jonathan presenting a seemingly inspirational address and the conference chairman Justice Kutigi accepting the burden of leadership with hopes of transforming the levers of the Nigerian society.

To be fair to the conference and its organizers it is my view that it was the most broad-minded and diverse in comparison to other conferences in terms of membership. There were seasoned politicians like Peter

Odili and Victor Attah, military-era generals like Ike Nwachukwu, Zamani Lekwot, Idada Ikponmwem, Jerry Useni, Alani Akirinade and Paul Omu, former failed coup plotters like Col. Tony Nyiam, former ex-convicts like Chief DSP Alamieyeseigha and Navy Commander Olabode George, seasoned administrators and professionals like Atedo Peterside and Mahmood Yakubu, radical human rights lawyers like Olisa Agbakoba and Femi Falana, resource control activists like Issac Osuoka and Ankio Briggs, democracy activists like Jaiye Gaskiya and Auwal Rafsanjani, recurrent controversial elders like Chief E.K. Clark and Prof. Jubril Aminu. There were also failed politicians like Don Etiebet and Adolphus Nwabara and recurring political decimals like Ebenezer Babatope, Prof. Jerry Gana, Richard Akinjide, Ibrahim Mantu, Ahmadu Ali, AK Horsfall, Florence Ita-Giwa and Segun Osoba. It will be fair to say that there were also patriotic intellectuals like Professors Anya O. Anya and Bolaji Akinyemi who still serve as the conference's vice chairman.

The broad nature of the conference also allowed for the representation of organizations like market women's associations, women in business, people with disability, religious organizations, Nigerians in Diaspora, civil society organizations, Nigerian university students, journalists, editors and newspaper owners all of who joined the well-known governmental and non-governmental structures of the Nigerian society like the political parties, geo-political zones, chieftaincy institutions, major and minor trade unions like the NLC and TUC. The millennium conference had 94 delegates more than Obasanjo's 2005 National Political Reform Conference (NPRC). Political parties had 44.4 percent reduction while CSOs and women groups (including WINBIZ and NAWOJ) each had 300% increase in membership. Nigeria Youth Organizations (including NANS) had an increased 55.5% participation, the physically challenged increased by 100% while a combination of professional organizations like the NBA, ICAN, NMA, ANAN, CIB etc with no representation in Obasanjo's NPRC now had a whopping 13 delegates in the confab. The judiciary and ALGON which had no official representatives in Obasanjo's NPRC also have 6 delegates each in the present confab.

There was an observed attempt at geo-political balancing – an attempt at treating equals equally in the volume of delegates without necessarily treating unequals unequally – some form of convoluted process of justice that seeks further explanation. The figure '6' became a magic figure representing General Abacha's six geo-political zones of the country. Still, as expected there were misgivings over the constitution of the conference. For example, some Muslim organizations complained of having lesser number of Muslim delegates than Christian ones while some 'small' ethnic nationalities like the Ogba in Rivers State grumbled about having no single delegate at the conference.

One of the high points of the ongoing conference was the committee stage when 20 sub-committees were set up to address issues challenging the Nigerian state and the masses. With due respect to the conference the committees were near-exhaustive. There were committees on devolution of power, political restructuring and forms of government, national security, environment, politics and governance, law, judiciary, human rights and legal reforms, social sector, transportation, science, technology and development, agriculture, civil society, labour and sports, public service, political parties and electoral matters, foreign policy and Diaspora matters, land tenure and national boundaries, economy, trade and investment, energy, religion, public finance and revenue, and lastly immigration.

You will all agree with me that if these committee issues were sorted out properly and resolutions implemented in a utilitarian fashion, Nigeria stands to rise to the its feet as the liberator of the black race; the economy stands to improve through the expansion of the middle class and the ordinary people will become more secure and productive. The ruling classes will simply be having fun without security challenges. Democracy will be deepened and lectures of this nature will be unnecessary. Maybe, every day will be Friday and we will thank God for it...and all we will be doing is minimal maintenance of our democracy architecture. But it hardly happens like this and the problems of this world do not come to an end all of a sudden.

Observations

Let me state that in all the committees I did not see anything related to education. I stand to be corrected. When I searched a little bit further I saw it under the committee on social sector. If agriculture and transportation could have committees assigned to them, why not education? This inadequate attention accorded this item could in the minimum imply that the philosophy of Nigeria's education, instructional content, the level of funding and students' enrolment, the quality of teaching, learning and research in our educational institutions are adequate and acceptable. If it were so why will students offer to school outside the shores of Nigeria even with increasing number of private nursery, primary, secondary and tertiary schools? If so why would a student graduate from a Nigerian university and remain dysfunctional in the labour market and to society at large? Maybe the education sector is not so much of an important item for discussion. But it is this overriding attention deficit over the years that have, maybe, transmogrified the minds of men into burning down schools and killing or kidnapping innocent students.

There was also this we-and-them mentality in the deliberations of the conference. If it is not between the North and the South, or the East and the West, it is between the majorities and the minorities. This was made manifest in sessions covering the setting of the rules of the house and when discussing certain contentious issues which were the primary reasons for the conference. In the face of parochial sentiments the popular two-thirds and simple majority patterns were not agreed to. Also set aside was the three-quarter (75%) house majority suggested by the Secretary Government of the Federation, Senator Ayim Pius Ayim. In the end of the house rules session a strange compromise of 70% majority was reached, simply because 70% happen to be the 'roundest' figure in between 2/3 and 3/4. The major plank of the initial controversy in the conference was that no participants from Nigeria's North and South divide wanted to be seen as weak. This 70% majority, as against simple or 2/3 majority inserted into the house rules was aimed at frustrating certain issues like fiscal federalism, power devolution, state police and states creation. It simply showed that primordial sentiments planted in the minds of regional representatives in the past by the colonial masters were still at work. Hence, who says that the confab was not programmed to fail right from the beginning? So, if the conferees knew this, why did they continue with the confabulation? So, Nigeria has become a country where people show their strengths by the volume of disagreements they get into.

Another observation is the number of committees. Having earlier stated that the constitution of the conference committees was near-exhaustive, it is pertinent to ask if the multitudes of committees are the problems with Nigeria. We know of problems of power devolution, of fiscal federalism, of maybe insecurity and of reduction of central financial leakages by the possible implementation of a part-time parliamentary system. The coup de grâce is - what are we doing with committees on social sector, environment, aviation, science and technology, agriculture, civil society, labour, economy, trade and investment, sports, public service and Diaspora at this point in our national life? Are these committees not harping on symptoms instead of the disease with the Nigerian state? Are these committees not propped up in order to muddle the basic ideas of the conference? Maybe it was done to enable every conferee belong to a committee. But must everyone belong to a committee in the first place? Must everyone make a contribution at the conference? Does everyone at the confab even know the fundamental problems with the country?

Another observation is the advanced age of the conference leadership. Like in past conferences this year's confab was trapped in a gerontocratic predicament. While there was increased number of young people in this conference, must the leadership of a conference of this nature be retired old men? Can you all imagine that while the conference was going on some sick and tired old conferees were said to have slept themselves to death. Of what use is dragging around a retired and tired old man in the name of a confab? Was it not the same old men through their actions and inactions while in public offices that kept this country the way it is today? Since when has a disease become a cure?

On the Ruling Class Crisis and the National Conference

It is my considered view that the Nigerian ruling class is deep in irresolvable crisis and has to bid for time. The national conference therefore had to be an avenue to attempt to exhaust the contradictions of ruling class factions where alternative dispute resolution strategies are subtly encouraged across fault lines. It has also become an avenue for recruiting un-committed and non-aligned elements into different ruling class factions.

But education is very key to the needed transformation of consciousness. Unfortunately education has been mangled not to adequately serve society and this is not necessarily a process made manifest only in Nigeria. Whereas in certain societies like those of the West the machinery of state through education encourage defenseless and pliable children to become victims of an absurd propaganda aimed at making them die for certain interests that are against their interests, in Africa poverty is unleashed on the mass of the population and the educational process is an underhand one for reclusion into the belief that salvation can only come when money can be misused and abused. On the contrary excruciating poverty is the needed tranquilizer for the ruling classes to continue to manipulate the electoral and thought processes of the society. This is the crux of the Nigerian crisis.

Permit me to say that it is impossible to deepen democracy without the economic content. Poverty must slide lower and inequality must take a different, but narrower shape. Less than 2% of Nigerians (most of who are public office holders) cannot own and control over 98% of the national wealth, while more than 98% of the citizens struggle daily to survive on less than 2% of the resources. We must find a way to decentralize economic opportunities and national resources in such a way as to bridge this widening inequality gap between the haves and the have-nots. It is the harmonization of the economic content of democracy that can deepen and sustain democratic culture and make it relevant to the hopes and aspirations of the citizenry. Yes, it is the liberation of the economic man that leaps him into the political man. Yes, the poor can only participate in politics as tools in the hands of manipulators. The day the poor rejects this status he will be making a revolution.

The diversification of the economy, the harmonization of pro-poor people's policies, the employment technological improvement and stabilization of fiscal discipline are important in maintaining proper democratic conduct. In this regime corruption is fixated and treasury leakages are under institutional control. Economic growth is easily reversed in the absence of diversification, technological improvements and productivity. A dip in commodity prices is enough to create imbalance. Additionally, the extractive sector can propel growth in the economy but does not directly create stable jobs. This has remained the bane of extractive economies which are rentier in nature like Nigeria's.

There is need to strengthen the mechanisms that create and sustain small and medium scale enterprises (SMEs). Nigeria has the highest volume of yearly labour market entrants in Africa and cannot afford to discount the importance of SMEs. Considering the fact that the only way to help the poor is to expand the middle class, there is need to provide social services and credit facilities that will support middle class contributions, ideas and SMEs. Our inability to do this has its social consequences, as an increasing volume of people will filter out into the lower classes enveloped by poverty and squalor. It is already happening with the rise in the army of unemployed and extreme youth poverty.

But young people do not just need jobs; they need better jobs to be fulfilled. They need a viable place in the production function of society. They need to get out of subsistent agriculture and marginal self-employment into the bigger picture, into real productivity. Institutional mechanisms have to ensure this, else we will be dealing with social explosions and insecurity of strange kinds like the Niger Delta and Boko Haram debacles.

With viable economic content institutions of governance will work with greater efficiency and maintain structures of society. The ability of government to foment a viable tax regime will increase citizens' Involvement in governance and reduce underrepresentation in the long run.

This issue of underrepresentation is important because the federal allocation regime has led to citizens' inability to control the levers of governance. With monthly federal allocation distributions the governments in the conflict zones of the country, for example, have been observed to have lost the ability to take taxes from the citizens, hence the masses of those regions are completely discounted in the power equation by the political class. Hence the political class meets the ordinary people every four years, bribe them to vote based on certain peripheral ethnic or religious considerations and when they lose elections, descend into inciting the unconscious lower classes into violence based on such considerations. After elections development in the areas like the North East is usually at the maximum abandoned or at the minimum trivialized.

Challenges before the National Conference

Firstly, the national conference has to be relevant to the hopes and aspirations of the Nigerian masses. Personality clashes, ego trips and ethnic manipulations are supposed to be discounted and the problems of Nigeria put on the front burner dispassionately. Can the conferees rise above parochial considerations and project the idea of the greatest good for the greatest number, while not forgetting minority opinions?

Secondly, the results of the deliberations of the confab are expected to be subjected to a referendum. But will the lame-duck national assembly allow this process to go through for the greater good of Nigeria? Can the president commit a kind of class suicide and sideline the national assembly (considering the assembly's pedigree of docility) in the process of instituting a referendum? Won't this amount to an illegality? With the absence of a credible voter's register and other electoral deficiencies, can a referendum adequately gauge the popular wishes of Nigerians?

Thirdly, what if a referendum is carried out; are there viable institutional mechanisms to implement the resolutions of the conference? Or will the conference end like past conferences, whose reports remain stuck in the archives of Nigeria's political history?

Fourthly, won't the national conference amount to a waste of time and resources in the end? Is it not the same people who destroyed the country that are conferring today? Are they really conferring to make it better? Make it better for whom?

Questions on Some Possible Conference Resolutions

Will the removal of the immunity clause from our statue books eliminate the impunity of public officials, and by reducing financial leakages deepen the economic content of our democracy? Is the retention of 13% revenue by derivation not antithetical to progress of our federalism? Will the resolutions lead to a shift in focus of agitations from the North East back to the Niger Delta area in the next few years? Will the trimming of Federal Government revenue share from 52% to 42% improve federalism and aid in deepening democracy? Won't such devolution of funds to state and local governments become an additional burden to the central government that is already weighed down by items on the exclusive list? Will increment in revenue from allocation to the states necessarily lead to development with the systematic corruption and recklessness in the states? Should the states who find it difficult to pay teachers' salaries regularly take on the additional responsibility of state police and survive the inherent challenges common with security? Should certain delegates vote to kill propositions on issues they are not vulnerable to or interested in? There are so many questions and there are many more in your hearts?

Conclusion

It is my view that the Nigerian ruling classes are definitely at war with the masses of the country and at games with themselves. Their weapons of war against the masses are poverty and hunger.

It is my view also that they need to be disarmed or liquidated. If this is to be done by class suicide, mass democratic actions or armed insurrections will be determined by a combination of the dynamics of history and the objective conditions of the Nigerian society.

If a fraction of the objective conditions are truly represented by the ongoing national conference then the country is on the path of achieving greatness through the institutionalization of justice, economic, social and cultural rights which are enshrined in various international instruments, such as the 1948 Universal Declaration of Human Rights and the 1966 International Covenant on Economic, Social and Cultural Rights. It is on note that the Declaration and Covenant provide for the justiciable rights to just and favorable conditions of work, join and form trade unions; protection of children, women, and the family; social security and adequate standard of living –adequate food, clothing and shelter; health; education; take part in cultural life, protection of indigenous peoples' and their environment, benefit from progress in science; protection of property rights, etc.

On the contrary, if governance is not willing to look in the direction of human survival and the promotion and protection of these international legal instruments, then the Nigerian state is inherently calling for a reformation in the minimum, and revolution at the maximum. Reformation could easily revert back to barbarism in the face primordial sentiments but a revolution will furnish society with a new thinking and a permanent overhaul of the social architecture of society.

Finally, it is important to note that Nigeria is not the ugliest country in the world in whatever ramification we deem it. On the contrary it is a country with a lot of yet-to-be-realized potentials. It is the realization of these potentials of Nigeria that the national conference has been debating since early this year. Like one of the conferees will say 'the national conference is an avenue for struggle'. It is an opportunity to struggle for a better future. Unfortunately Nigeria has lost some impetus as we are going into the election year promising of serious decline in morality, of a rise in electoral violence, Boko

Haram audacity, and intervention of foreign forces in the fight against terror and sundry manifestations of violence.

In the face of these challenges many will say Nigeria is moving towards being classified as a failed country. I respect their sentiments but strongly believe there is hope. It is this remnant hope that made me travel from Port Harcourt to Awka without fear of anything or anybody. It is this hope that kept us together for more than one hour now. With this hope I say; we as a people must rise up and reclaim our country and further help Nigeria take its place in history as the liberator of the black race.

Thank you.

Appendix 1

Full text of President Jonathan's address at inauguration of National Conference.

PROTOCOLS

1. I am delighted to welcome you all to the inauguration of this historic National Conference which promises to be another significant landmark in our efforts to strengthen national unity and consolidate democratic governance in our beloved country.

2. I also believe that this National Conference is coming at a very appropriate time. Having just celebrated the first centenary of our country, the most compelling task before us, as we move ahead and contemplate what our nation will be at the end of its second century, is to lay a much stronger foundation for faster development.

3. This we can achieve by building a more inclusive national consensus on the structure and guiding principles of state that will guarantee our emergence as a more united, progressive and prosperous nation.

4. In our history as a political entity, we have experienced highs and lows but have always forged ahead. To my mind, the fact that we have weathered all storms and continued with the mission of evolving a

truly national identity signifies that we are going in the right direction.

5. The strongest nations in the world today also went through their own formative stages; some for decades and others for centuries. We must learn from them that nationhood will not happen overnight, especially given the circumstances of our birth as a nation.

6. History also teaches that nation-building is a journey of dedication, commitment, diligence, perseverance and patriotic vision. To be successful, nation-builders must continually strive to evolve better and more inclusive societies in which every citizen is a proud and committed stakeholder.

7. It was with this objective in mind that we set up the Presidential Advisory Committee (PAC) on the National Conference in October last year and charged its members with the responsibility of designing the framework and modalities for a productive National Conference.

8. The Committee which submitted its Report in December, 2013, was able to reach out to all Nigerians and various interest groups, socio-political groupings, regional and religious elements, professionals, civil society, the organised private sector, labour, youth,

women and others to ascertain their views on the initiative.

9. The Presidential Advisory Committee established that there was indeed, a national consensus for this Conference to be convened immediately, to meet the yearnings and aspirations of our people.

10. The National Conference is therefore being convened to engage in intense introspection about the political and socio-economic challenges confronting our nation and to chart the best and most acceptable way for the resolution of such challenges in the collective interest of all the constituent parts of our fatherland.

11. This coming together under one roof to confer and build a fresh national consensus for the amicable resolution of issues that still cause friction amongst our people must be seen as an essential part of the process of building a more united, stronger and progressive nation.

12. We cannot continue to fold our arms and assume that things will straighten themselves out in due course, instead of taking practical steps to overcome impediments on our path to true nationhood, rapid development and national prosperity.

13. For many years we have discussed and argued over various issues concerning our national existence and

well-being. Much of this national discourse has been conducted through the mass media, both print and electronic. More recently, the advent of the age of ICT and social media has greatly enlarged the space for the discussion of our country's future.

14. Many more young and articulate Nigerians who previously had little access to the traditional mass media have now joined the conversation, motivated by patriotic concern for good governance, peace, stability, justice, equity, fairness and the harmonious co-existence of the diverse groups that make up our great nation.

15. Dear Compatriots, my administration is convening this National Conference today because we believe that we must assume responsibility for ensuring that the long-running national debate on the best way forward for our country is not in vain.

16. It is our expectation that participants in this conference will patriotically articulate and synthesize our peoples' thoughts, views and recommendations for a stronger, more united, peaceful and politically stable Nigeria, forge the broadest possible national consensus in support of those recommendations, and strive to ensure that they are given the legal and constitutional backing to shape the present and the future of our beloved fatherland.

17. In inaugurating this national conference today, we are not unmindful of the argument of those who say that we do not need such a conference since we already have an elected Parliament and an elected Government in place.

18. As cogent as that argument may sound, I have chosen to act on the sincere conviction that in the truly democratic nation we are striving to build, we must never ignore the loudly expressed views of the majority of ordinary Nigerians.

19. I have heard that majority say, that we need to rebuild trust by involving them in the process of developing a guiding document of our national political relationships which is more acceptable to all sections of the country. I have heard our people say that we need to openly and frankly discuss our problems and seek acceptable solutions instead of allowing them to fester and remain sources of perennial conflict.

20. I have also heard them say that, as the elected representatives of our people, we must never arrogate to ourselves all knowledge and wisdom regarding the development of our country.

21. And I am in full agreement with our people. The power we hold is, without question, in trust for the people. Sovereignty belongs to the people. Their voices

must be heard and factored into every decision we take on their behalf.

22. This National Conference is a very important avenue for the voices of our people to be heard. Our people have yearnings and desires that need to be discussed. Their representatives at this conference are neither usurping the role of the National Assembly nor the Executive. They are complementing us in our march towards a greater and stronger union.

23. Over the years, well-meaning Nigerians have drawn attention to inadequacies in our current constitution. Some have described it as a military-inspired document which does not take into full consideration the genuine desires and wishes of the people.

24. The phrase in the preamble that says "we, the people," has been variously criticised as being misleading because, according to the critics, the constitution was not written by the people. There are also those who believe that the constitution is not our problem but the political will to faithfully implement it for the peace and progress of Nigeria.

25. While opinions on the matter can be as diverse as rain showers, I believe that irrespective of our personal views on the issue, no one can deny the fact that every constitution is a living document that needs to be

revised and improved upon from time to time. The United States, which is the model democracy in the eyes of many, has amended its constitution 27 times since it was first adopted in 1787.

26. Some of our compatriots also believe that because we have held several conferences in the past, we do not need to hold another one. I do not share that view at all.

27. A deeper look will reveal that the challenges we faced before each of the preceding national conferences were different. The challenges of 1956 are certainly not the challenges of 2014, and definitely not the challenges that the nation will face in years to come. It makes sense, therefore, that as the challenges before us evolve, we must be constant and proactive in our search for fresh solutions. We cannot continue to proffer yesterday's solutions for today's problems.

28. This conference is open for us to table our thoughts and positions on issues, and make recommendations that will advance our togetherness. The issues range from form of government, structures of government, devolution of powers, revenue sharing, resource control, state and local government creation, boundary adjustment, state police and fiscal federalism, to local government elections, indigeneship, gender equality and children's rights, amongst others.

29. We must not approach these issues with suspicion and antagonism. Rather, we should be open-minded and work to achieve what is best for Nigeria. Even though you come to the Conference as nominees and representatives of different interest groups, I urge you all to make a more united, stronger, indivisible and prosperous Nigeria your preoccupation and reference point at this national gathering. Whatever the pressures on you may be, I call upon you to put the best interest of Nigeria before all other sectional or group interests.

30. Indeed, I am quite worried when I hear people say that some participants in this National Conversation are coming here to defend and promote ethnic or clannish agenda. It is very regrettable that there are persons who believe that we cannot undertake any collective task in our country without the hindrance of ethnic rivalry even after 100 years of nationhood.

31. This conference gives us an opportunity to prove such persons wrong and I believe it will. As we start a new century of nationhood, we have an obligation to reshape and redirect our country for the benefit of our children. There should be no room for divisive cleavages and ethnic jingoism. There should be no room for selfish considerations that defeat the purpose of national progress. There should be room only for the national interest.

32. In the 60s, our country was ranked along with some developing countries including India, Malaysia and South Korea. Today, those countries have moved far ahead of us in several areas. My expectation is that the outcome of this Conference will be a positive turning point for our country's development. We must seize this opportunity to cement the cleavages and fault lines that tend to separate us. We must re-launch our country.

33. I know the task before you is onerous; but there must be only one winner, and there can only be one winner if we do everything right, and that winner must be Nigeria. I urge you therefore to focus strictly on the Nigerian Agenda.

34. I expect that, as persons of integrity and honour, you will do nothing in this Conference that will undermine our efforts and desire to build a truly great nation. I also expect that your discussions will be informed only by the noblest of instincts and persuasions.

35. Our sole motivation for convening this conference is the patriotic desire for a better and greater nation. We are determined that things must be done in a way and manner that will positively advance that objective.

36. While we recognise that groups and communities are the building blocks of our nation, we must also

emphasize that we need one another to build the solid and prosperous country of our dreams.

37. We cannot join hands together to build with a collective vision if we continue to harbour negative biases and prejudices against ourselves.

38. Yesterday's prejudices should die with yesterday. Today is a new day. This is the dawn of a new era. This is an opportunity to think anew. We must jettison the poisonous mind-sets of the past, which were built on unhealthy competition among our diverse groups and peoples.

39. We need a new mind and a new spirit of oneness and national unity. The time has come to stop seeing Nigeria as a country of many groups and regions. We have been divinely brought together under one roof. We must begin to see ourselves as one community. We are joined together by similar hopes and dreams as well as similar problems and challenges. What affects one part of the community affects the other.

40. An average Nigerian sees every part of the country as home. Let us seize the opportunity of this Conference to do more to further turn our diversity and plurality into unique national resources for strength and greatness.

41. I have always affirmed that our ability to stay together despite our acknowledged differences, when

other countries are finding it difficult to meet that challenge, is a powerful statement by Nigeria to the world on the virtues of tolerance and unity.

42. It is a strong and compelling statement in a world much afflicted by strife and violence. We must sustain it. We must not allow the antagonists of unity and togetherness to prevail. We must work ceaselessly to remain one nation bound in freedom, peace and unity, as our National Anthem says.

43. Honourable Chairman and distinguished delegates, I urge you not to be under any illusions as you begin your assignment. The task that lies ahead of you is formidable. Over the coming weeks, you will be confronted with complex and emotive issues; strong views will be expressed by opposing sides and some disagreements will, in all likelihood, be intense.

44. I sincerely believe, however, that we can overcome all obstacles to true national unity if we dig deep into the recesses of our national character and look up to God Almighty for wisdom, guidance and the generosity of spirit we need to ensure the success of this conference.

45. Once again, I wish to express my appreciation to the Nigerian people who have, without hesitation, accepted dialogue as a means of resolving all differences and tensions that may exist in the country, and therefore,

given their unequivocal support for this National Conference.

46. Let me at this point thank the National Assembly for introducing the provision for a referendum in the proposed amendment of the Constitution. This should be relevant for this Conference if at the end of the deliberations, the need for a referendum arises. I therefore urge the National Assembly and the State Houses of Assembly to speed up the Constitutional amendment process especially with regard to the subject of referendum.

47. I thank the Chairman, Senator Femi Okurounmu and members of the Presidential Advisory Committee for the arduous work they undertook to prepare for the Conference. I also thank the Chairman of this National Conference, Justice Idris Legbo Kutigi, the principal officers and all the distinguished patriots and representatives of our people who have taken time off their busy personal schedules to serve the cause of national unity and progress at this conference.

48. I am confident that we are embarking on a landmark journey that will make us stronger as a nation if we undertake it with all sense of purpose and sincerity. Let us do that which is selfless, purposeful and patriotic so that history will remember us for having served our nation well.

49. In conclusion, I urge all officials and participants in the national conference to work extra hard to ensure that their deliberations are completed on schedule, well ahead of the schedule of events for the next general elections already announced by the Independent National Electoral Commission (INEC).

50. Let me again repeat what I have been saying that Goodluck Jonathan has no personal agenda in convening this national conference.

51. Ladies and Gentlemen, I now have the honour and privilege of declaring the National Conference open, for the good of our Nation and to the glory of God Almighty who has brought us together.

52. I thank you all.

Appendix 2

Speech by Hon. Justice Idris Legbo Kutigi, GCON, FNIALS, FCIArb, FNJI, (Former Chief Justice of the Supreme Court of Nigeria) Chairman, National Conference at the Occasion of the Submission of the 2014 National Conference Report in Abuja, Nigeria, 21 August, 2014

Protocol

Mr. President, when you inaugurated the 2014 National Conference on 17 March, 2014, we knew that we were taking on a tough assignment. If truth be told, most Nigerians did not believe that this whole enterprise was going to last this long or come to a successful conclusion.

2. Yet, Mr. President, here we are five months later at a ceremony to mark the successful execution of our mandate.

3. It is not that we lasted this long that is newsworthy; but that we overcame all the obstacles in our way.

4. Mr. President, when 494 Nigerians are assembled to address the fears, disappointments, aspirations and hopes which have accumulated over one hundred years, it is only to be expected that the debates would be robust; and indeed the debates were robust. It was only

to be expected that tempers would fly; and tempers did fly.

5. Mr. President, we did not try to ignore or bury our differences. We addressed these differences while respecting the dignity of those holding these differences and sought to construct solutions which would become building blocks for a just and stable nation.

6. Mr. President, we approved over 600 resolutions; some dealing with issues of law, issues of policy and issues of constitutional amendments. These resolutions did not deal with frivolous or inconsequential issues. We showed courage in tackling substantial and fundamental issues.

7. Mr. President, time will not permit me to list all the critical and fundamental resolutions adopted. But let me emphasize this: all our resolutions were adopted by consensus. Not once did we have to vote or come to a division. This is a message that we wish the world to hear loud and clear. Nigerians are capable of not only discussing their differences but are also capable to coming up with solutions to these difficulties.

8. Mr. President, the magnitude of what we have done is reflected in our Report and Annexures of 22 volumes of approximately 10,335 (ten thousand, three hundred and thirty-five) pages. Mr. President, the official Report of

the 2014 National Conference was also adopted unanimously.

9. In the post-independence history of Nigeria, there have been four Conferences, including this 2014 National Conference. However, Mr. President, our own task has been the most arduous. The following statistics graphically illustrates this. The 1978 Constituent Assembly had a membership of 230 people and met for 9 months. The 1995 National Constitutional Conference had a membership of 371 people and met for twelve (12) months. The 2005 National Political Reform Conference was made up of 400 delegates and met for 5 months. We are 494 in membership and you made us do all this work in 4½ months.

10. Lasting Impression: On behalf of the delegates to the 2014 National Conference, I thank you for your courage in summoning this Conference. We have finally laid to rest the apprehension that a National Conference will lead to the disintegration of Nigeria. We have held a National Conference and we are more united today than ever.

11. Let me state here categorically and with the fear of Almighty Allah in my heart, that not once did you interfere or dictate to us in the course of this Conference. The only time we tried to consult the President during the conflict over voting percentages at

the very beginning of the Conference we were told that the issue was for us to resolve. At no time after that did you meet with us or speak to us.

12. I also wish to thank my fellow members of the Conference Management and Conference delegates for the vibrant, even if at times turbulent, cooperation in ensuring a successful Conference.

13. I thank especially the former and present Administrator of the National Judicial Institute and their staff for their contribution to the success of this 2014 National Conference. Mr. President, let it be on record that all these facilities were turned over to us with less than 12hrs notice.

14. I thank all of you who have responded positively by accepting our invitation to attend this closing ceremony. Your presence has added gravitas to this ceremony.

15. At this juncture, I want to convey to the National Assembly, the greatest respect of all members of the 2014 National Conference. We accept that the National Assembly has a pivotal role to play in ensuing that the Conference Report translates into law.

16. Mr. President, please permit me to pay tribute to four of our delegates who died during the pendency of the Conference. Barrister Hamma Misau who died on March 27; Dr. Mohammad Jumare who died on May 5;

Professor Dora Akunyili, on June 7; and Professor Mohammad Nur Alkali, on August 1, 2014. May their souls rest in peace.

17. Finally, Mr. President, let me on behalf of all of us thank the Secretary to Government, Senator Anyim Pius Anyim, GCON, who went beyond the call of duty in virtually turning over all the facilities of Government to assist this Conference.

18. And now on behalf of the 2014 National Conference and the people of Nigeria, I hereby present to your Excellency, President Goodluck Ebele Jonathan, GCFR, President of the Federal Republic of Nigeria, 21 Volumes of the Report of the 2014 National Conference. Here, Mr. President is the Main Report and on that table are the remaining 19 Volumes of supporting documents.

Thank you.

Hon. Justice Idris Legbo Kutigi, GCON,FNIALS,FCIrb,FNJI

(Former Chief Justice of Nigeria)

Chairman, National Conference – 2014

August 21, 2014.

www.ingramcontent.com/pod-product-compliance
Lightning Source LLC
Chambersburg PA
CBHW071119280526
45787CB00003B/1099